Upbringing

poems

Marian Kaplun Shapiro

Plain View Press, LLC
1101 W 34th Street, STE 404

www.plainviewpress.com
Austin, TX 78705

Copyright © 2023 Marian Kaplun Shapiro. All rights reserved under International and Pan-American Copyright Conventions. No part of this book may be reproduced or distributed in any form or by any means, or stored in a data base or retrieval system, without written permission from the author. All rights, including electronic, are reserved by the author and publisher.

ISBN: 978-1-63210-097-9
Library of Congress Control Number: 2022942372

Cover Art: Photograph by George Campbell
Digital Artist and Computer Guru: David Shapiro
Cover Design: Pam Knight

We Find Healing In Existing Reality

Plain View Press is a 47-year-old issue-based literary publishing house. Our books result from artistic collaboration between writers, artists, and editors. Over the years we have become a far-flung community of humane and highly creative activists whose energies bring humanitarian enlightenment and hope to individuals and communities grappling with the major issues of our time—peace, justice, the environment, education and gender.

To Irwin,
my forever husband whom I married
on the rim of childhood, at age 20,
when he had just turned 30.
Now we are in our eighties and nineties.
All that love! How lucky I have been.

Contents

Oh Freedom   9
Introduction   11

Section 1: Innocence   13

Maternity   15
Bill of Rights for New Parents   16
Bill of Rights for the Newborn   17
Discipline 101   18
Daddy   19
First Homonym   20
Babysitter   21
Always Tell the Truth #1: Innocence   22
Always Tell the Truth #2: New Friend   23
Always Tell the Truth #3: Shopping While Black   24
The Moment Everything Changed   25
Identity   26
Vocation   27
Gender   28
Always Tell the Truth #4: How Old Are You?   29
Song   30
Introduction to Euphemism   31
A Shocking Discovery   32
Always Tell the Truth #5: Oh Vanity   33
Welcome   34
Baby at Home   35
Overheard   36
Moving to an Apartment (Two Perspectives)   37
Three Strikes Is Out: Strike One   38
Three Strikes Is Out: Strike Two   39

Section 2: The Big Question Mark	**41**
Three Strikes Is Out: Strike Three	43
Do As I Say…	44
Vaccination	45
Self-Defense on the Playground	46
Beauty Lesson	47
Fairy Tale	48
NOT Happily Ever After	49
He loves me, he loves me not	50
An Unbelievable Scene That Happened (Part 1)	51
An Unbelievable Scene That Happened (Part 2)	52
First Day of Kindergarten	53
Teaching Generosity	54
Friend	55
Freedom of Choice	56
A Day Off From School	57
Ethical Dilemma (Age 6)	58
Learning My Colors at Breakfast	59
Timing	60
Sticks and Stones	61
Introduction to Religion	62
The Teacher Is Always Right	63
Preparation for Life	64
Attachment, Scrambled	65
Fame/Honor/Glory/Death	66
Always Tell the Truth #6: Home Alone	67
Those Who Are 10 Are Not 40.	
Those Who Are 40 Are Not 10.	68
Bully	69
God, #1	70
God, #2	71
Justice	72
Attempted Rape	73

Studying the Constitution	74
Genes at the Passover Seder	75
Avoidant Attachment Disorder: A Simple Illustration	76
Reputation	77
Said Without Thinking, Thinking Without Saying	78
A Slippery Definition	79
Scripture	80
Father-Son Lecture	81
Always Tell the Truth #7: (Not) Just What I Wanted	82
Music Class	83
Tattling	84
The Perils of Being Praised by the Teacher	85
Secret Wishes	86
Lesson From the Coach: How To Score	87
Not Coming Out	88
Coming of Age	89
Being Beautiful	90
Maternal Advice	91
Soap Opera Meets Real Life	92
The Facts of Life	93
Surprise	94
Endpaper	95
YOU	96

About the Author 97

Oh Freedom

You all know this place, the prison
of your childhood. You demur—it
wasn't bad; it wasn't SO bad; it was,
even, a good childhood. I'm glad for you,
for you who have no memories you had to change/
forget/deny/excuse: I met one such person in
my now extremely long lifetime. If you,
lucky you, were resident of the loveliest of homes,
the kindest of parents, the most benevolent
of teachers, the most open-hearted, open-minded
adults you counted on, even you would not have been
free to leave, likely not even free to choose your breakfast.
Not really. Peanut butter and jelly? That's lunch, not breakfast.
Cheerios or Cornflakes, dear?

You know that freedom
is what children learn to lose,
one way or the other.

You all know this truth, and knowing it,
you sigh with resignation. It is what it is,
you say. We grow up anyway. We plant our flower gardens,
rows of crocuses, of daffodils, sunflowers, tulips, roses...
predetermined to appear according to our plans.
Our children come along, another generation,
tiny prisoners of whom we have become the guards.
Are there little spaces in which some weeds might grow?
Weeds we can call wildflowers?

Introduction

How simple it is to damage—even destroy—a work of art. By accident, by ignorance, by carelessness—not to mention by intent. An etched glass vase is dropped—shattered. Unrepairable. A painting smudged by dirt. A drop of ink, or coffee, or—god forbid—of red wine. A rip caused by a roughness of skin. Perhaps years of expert attention can undo a moment's damage.

Each human being is a unique, priceless work of art. Being helpless to survive on their own for many years, unlike all other animals, we babies are 'raised' by ex-babies who were 'raised' by yet another set of ex-babies—and so on, world without end. Damage occurs. Guaranteed. Like art, some can be repaired, some cannot be. Some damage is visible, some not. Some cracks, some splotches may even make the result more beautiful. And often the repair makes for greater structural integrity than the original. But always, I believe, the noticing, the understanding of the process of the creation of damage and its outcomes is vitally important to the result. I suppose that's why I became a psychologist—one who studies the soul, with the hope of helping to assist in its restoration.

These pages you turn hold poems. No, most of these poems don't present in lines, with carefully curated rhythms and stunning images made of words. As graphic poems, being poems, they head for essence. In my doctoral thesis I addressed the effect of low-syllable words in speech and writing: The greater the percentage of one-syllable words, the more powerful the feeling behind the communication. BECAUSE that is the language of the child. Before the child has learned to hide, to obfuscate—to LIE successfully. It is to those children, who had to surrender themselves to please their caretakers, and to join their society, that I have written this book of poems. It is for you.

One last note about this book. Your book. I hope you will write, draw, and COLOR the images and words as you feel them. Really. And as for coloring outside the lines? In the margins? I have, have I not? Keep me company!

Section 1: Innocence

Innocence—the era before you knew that you didn't know (Identity; Always Tell The Truth: Innocence; Song). Others, once innocent, tell you, but you thank them politely, and go on your innocent way into the hurricane without your extra lanterns and your store of batteries and cans. Next time a storm threatens, at least you'll know you didn't know (Introduction To Euphemism). Sometimes you suspect, beginning to collect information, develop the germs of strategies (Always Tell The Truth, #2: New Friend;) Now you'll listen to the experts, those who came before weathered the emergencies and lived. Someday you'll be one of them. Someday you too will forget that pure, beautiful, and dangerous state you might not have survived.

Maternity

"Rock-a-bye baby ♫ ♪
on the treetop
When the wind blows
the cradle will rock,"

"When the bough breaks
The cradle will FALL,
Down will come baby
cradle and all."

Oh no — What did I sign up for!

Bill of Rights for New Parents

It's ok
that you don't know.
Learn from the one who knows what your baby needs.
You know who that is.
Listen. Look.
When you can, sleep.

Bill of Rights for the Newborn

I am.
Whoever I am, I am.
You may not try to convince me otherwise.
I am yours—to love.
Yours to listen to.
Yours to discover, to help, to delight in,
as I am.

Discipline 101

If you don't stop crying, I'll give you something to cry about.

Daddy

THE POLICE SAY YOU BEAT YOUR BABY BOY LAST NIGHT. CAN YOU TELL ME ABOUT THAT?

So what, big deal. He was crying and crying and he wouldn't stop after I told him I had a really hard day, and besides my father beat me and it didn't do me no harm. Taught me a lesson! People these days they're a bunch of wimps.

TELL ME ABOUT YOUR FATHER.

What for? He's dead, that bastard.

HOW ABOUT YOUR MOTHER?

Keep her outa this, no one gonna dis my mother, you bitch.

SO MR. JONES, HOW ABOUT I SET YOU UP WITH A COUNSELOR FOR ANGER MANAGEMENT?

Nah, forget it. Waste of time. I'm just a bad guy. Always will be.

WHY DO YOU SAY THAT??

My father said so. That's why he beat me, see?

What an asshole, that lady

Another lost cause

First Homonym

Babysitter

Good evening, Mrs. O'Neill, right on time as usual!

Hello, folks, going out to dinner tonight?

Yes, we're going to the movies afterwards, so we'll be home around midnight, is that ok for you?

Oh yes, I'll play with Donny here for a while, and then off to bed with him.

Oh Donny don't cry, you like Mrs. O'Neill.

No no no no NO
(No I don't she smells funny she just watches tv, she doesn't play with me, she isn't gentle)

I'm sorry, Mrs. O'Neill, I guess he's just in the NO stage.

Always Tell the Truth #1: Innocence

Mimi, this is Mrs. Brown. She's going to be your babysitter today.

Is your name Mrs. Brown because you are brown?

MIMI! DON'T BE SO RUDE! I'm so sorry Mrs. Brown!

(thought bubble: Why was that rude?)

Always Tell the Truth #2: New Friend

Lucy, Mrs. Wilson and I are going to have tea in the kitchen, and you and Rosie can get to know each other.

Wow Rosie, you are so fat!

LUCY! THAT IS VERY RUDE! You hurt her feelings!

But she is very fat.

NEVER COMMENT ON SOMEONE ELSE'S BODY!

Ok, the rule is don't say anything about anyone's body.

Always Tell the Truth #3: Shopping While Black

> Doesn't this dress look great on your Mommy?

NO.

> Sure it does, Look at the pretty flowers on it. Your mommy is just the right color for it, it's like flowers growing in the dirt, I mean in the EARTH.

I don't like it and I don't like YOU!

> You are a stupid ugly little girl.

> DON'T YOU THROW THOSE CLOTHES ON THE FLOOR!

NO ONE TALKS TO MY DAUGHTER LIKE THAT! WE'RE GETTING OUTTA HERE RIGHT NOW AND REPORTING YOU TO THE CHAMBER OF COMMERCE.

COME ON, SWEETIE, I'M PROUD OF YOU!

But I DID throw the clothes on the floor...

The Moment Everything Changed

"No child of MINE would..."

SHE'S NOT MY MOTHER?

who IS my mother,

Identity

"Who do you think you are!!"

(I know that one)

I'm Jimmy Rosco
I live at 155 Chestnut Street
In Acton, Massachusetts
My phone number is–

I forgot, Mom!

"DON'T BE FRESH.
Get to your room and write
I will not be fresh to my
mother 100 times."

"Make that 150 times...."

? But Mom–

!

Vocation

When I grow up I'm going to be a TRUCK DRIVER!

Oh no dear, you are going to be a doctor, just like your daddy.

OK, MOM —

Maybe she'll let me be a doctor who drives a truck!

Gender

"REAL BOYS DON'T PLAY WITH DOLLS."

But I play with dolls, and I'm a boy—

and I'm real, aren't I?

Always Tell the Truth #4: How Old Are You?

Here we are, now I will get the tickets. You just stand here while I buy them.

Two, please, one adult and one under five, yes, she's 4 ½.

OF COURSE I DIDN'T FORGET! IT COSTS MORE IF YOU ARE FIVE. IT'S RIDICULOUS TO PAY MORE. YOU TAKE UP THE SAME SEAT WE ARE PAYING FOR.

Sorta, but everybody does it. Like saying FINE when someone asks how are you, you don't start telling them about all your little problems.

Song

♫   ♪
Oh you get the same milk from a brown skinned cow, ♪
♪ ♪   The color of the skin doesn't matter no how…

> Mommy, what does that mean?

That means I am going to school to talk to your principal! No one is going to teach that communist garbage to my kid.

> But I like that song, It has a good rhyme.

You'll understand when you get older. How about singing *You Are My Sunshine!*

Introduction to Euphemism

A Shocking Discovery

What was on the news tonight?

Oh, the usual lies. The governor said he didn't you know what and the woman is lying. Likewise the British prince. The senator said he always votes his conscience, nothing to do with his investments—hah. And of course the former President repeats his lies about winning the election which he lost. The only true news was the big snowstorm on 95, people stuck there for hours.

Oh yes, all the time. All of them lie, but some of them lie more than others.

Dear, do you think he's old enough for such a conversation?

This is his world, he has to learn. It wasn't just a story, it was a deliberate lie, to make Washington look good.

Don't worry about it, dear, when you are grown up you'll understand all of this stuff. You'll get used to it like everyone does.

Always Tell the Truth #5: Oh Vanity

I got a fabulous dress for the wedding at half price! It makes me look so young! What do you think, dear, doesn't it look great on me?

Very nice.

Oh you men, you don't really appreciate fashion. I bet our daughter has a more developed sense of clothes than you have! Lucy, what do you think, doesn't this dress make me look, like, 30? Really, I want you to tell me the truth.

> No, I think a mini looks silly on you, your legs have all those veins, and –

STOP THAT RIGHT NOW! "IF YOU HAVEN'T GOT SOMETHING NICE TO SAY DON'T SAY ANYTHING AT ALL." *Remember that?*

> Oops—I mentioned her legs—I got another rule. Don't believe anyone who says they want you to tell them the truth about their body.

Welcome

Mandy! Something exciting is going to happen!

WHAT MOMMY? AM I GETTING A PRESENT?

Yes, you're getting a baby sister!

WILL I LIKE HER?

Oh yes, she will be your sister.
She won't be able to play for a while, but
as she gets older, she will be able to talk and play with you.
You were once a baby too. And now you are three, you are a big girl.

So we have another present for you—a real big girl bed!
Babies have to sleep in a crib, so now you can give the crib
to baby, and sleep in the real bed.

BUT I LIKE MY CRIB AND SO DOES MY DOLLY!

Don't be selfish. You'll get used to it, don't worry, so will your dolly.

I'M NOT SELFISH, I'M SCARED!

???

Are you crying? Why are you crying, Mandy?

Baby at Home

Come here, Janie, come see how cute Wendy
looks in your old onesie!

NOT NOW, MOMMY.
I'M BUSY.

Oh, come on, she's in your old crib, with your
old baby blanket, it's so adorablve

NO THANKS, MOM,
DOLLY NEEDS HER BOTTLE.

What's the matter with that kid! I thought she'd enjoy being the big
sister!

Overheard

So the funniest thing, I have to tell you...

???

This morning when I came downstairs, I found Janie standing in the livingroom with her little red wheelie, holding her favorite dolly. I said, Are you going, somewhere, Janie? And she said, I'm going to grandma's.

??? Doesn't your mother live in California?

Right, but you know, on Zoom everyone's in the same little squares, Near or far, makes no difference, kids don't have any idea of distance. So I said, That's nice dear, how come you're going to see her? Do you miss your grandma? And she said I don't want to live here anymore, I don't like it here, you and daddy aren't nice to me, and you are always yelling at each other. So goodbye! And out she went, marching down the street. Of course she came back in a few minutes. Crying.

What did you do then?

Oh well, I gave her a Kleenex, and some milk and a cookie, and told her to go to her room and think about what she did, and when she was ready she could come out and apologize. Kids! It'll blow over. Then there'll be something else.

But really, she must've looked so cute with that suitcase and her doll—

Moving to an Apartment (Two Perspectives)

Well, hon, you'll get to see our new apartment tomorrow. You'll get used to living in the city, even though you'll miss all the grass and trees out here.

I love cities - so many playgrounds

What's an uh-partment?

It's a kinda house in a big tall building with lots of other people in their own apartments. There is an elevator, and there are people who live in apartments next to you, over you and under you too. Sometimes it is noisy because people are yelling, or playing the piano, or playing their tvs really loud. And there are lots of kids making noise.

That Sounds Exciting!

An elevator! Can I push the buttons?

Yes, I will show you how. We will live on the 14th floor.

Wow, that is high! I can count to 14, wanna hear?
1, 2, 3, 4, 5, 6, 7, 8, 9, 10, 11, 12, 13, 14!

Remember, there will be lots of people, and some of them won't be nice, and lots and lots of kids, and some of them won't be like your friends here, they speak all kinds of languages, like Korean, some of them won't like you because you are brown, and some of them don't have a lot of toys, and some of them will try to take your toys and be mean to you.

Don't worry, Mommy, I know how to share. And I like noise. And lots of the kids will like me.

How does Hi sound in KOREAN??

Three Strikes Is Out: Strike One

Mother's Day is like a birthday—You get Mommy a present and you wrap it all nicely, and give it to her and say Happy Mother's Day, NOT Happy Birthday.

I found a really pretty bracelet in Mommy's drawer, and I took a paper towel, and drew a picture on it and wrapped up the bracelet, and scotch taped it closed, and gave it to Mommy.

What the ❓

It's my own bracelet ! You stole my own bracelet from my drawer and gave it to me as a PRESENT !

I can't believe you can be so stupid ! Put it back in my drawer and repeat after me: I'M SORRY, MOMMY, I WILL NEVER STEAL YOUR THINGS AGAIN.

Three Strikes Is Out: Strike Two

Mother's Day is like a birthday—You get Mommy a present and you wrap it all nicely, and give it to her and say Happy Mother's Day, NOT Happy Birthday. And you can't take something out of her drawer.

So I am going to make a bracelet for mommy. I have a nice red rubber band and I will put a shiny paper clip on it like a diamond. Now I wrap it in aluminum foil. It will look so pretty that way.

What is it?

    A diamond bracelet ! Put it on, Mommy!

OW!!
That paper clip is sharp. You can't give someone a present that hurts. And it is NOT a diamond, it is a paper clip. Throw it in the trash immediately before it hurts someone else.

Section 2:
The Big Question Mark

What is a lie? When is it ok to lie? Why is it ok or not ok? When is it ok to break a promise? When is it the right thing to do to be a 'snitch'? How do you deal with a mean 'friend'? What is a friend, anyway? And what happens when you die? And what/who is God that allows cruelty, unfairness, and tragedy on earth?

You notice all those question marks. After the era of innocence arrives the era of the question. The child really wants to know—it's not the reflexive why why why—in fact, many of those are real questions too. Because I say so says the frustrated parent, but actually, the parent is frustrated because they can't really articulate the answer, if they even know it, in a way that the child can make use of it. These are big questions. And, in the long run children learn to adopt the attitude of the adults—or the opposite—in which these questions and their answers or non-answers sink below the surface of their practical lives.

So, they negotiate their lives, as their parents did before them. Much of their conclusions occur inwardly, as in the thought balloons. Feelings, compromises, decisions, most shared with nobody. Sometimes they give up (Strike Three) (Said Without Thinking), permanently or temporarily. Sometimes the direction of their life is set for good (God, #1) or evil (Preparation for Life) (Bully); for tragedy (Justice); depression (Attachment, scrambled) (Said Without Thinking); for self-determination (Maternal Advice) (Freedom of Choice). Everyone does life in their own unique way. You have your stories, as I have mine. The time when....

Three Strikes Is Out: Strike Three

Mother's Day is like a birthday—You get Mommy a present and you wrap it all nicely, and give it to her and say Happy Mother's Day, NOT Happy Birthday. And don't take something out of her drawer. And nothing sharp. And no diamonds.

So daddy had a good idea. He gave me some money and took me to the CVS and let me pick a bracelet. I picked a gold one without any diamonds and I was careful that there was nothing sharp on it. They wrapped it in CVS paper with hearts on it too. I hope Mommy will like this one—I felt like giving up, but daddy said to give it one more try like the three strikes in baseball. Sometimes the third try is a home run !

From CVS?

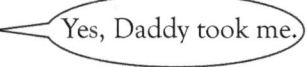

Well, you'll just have to take it back, this isn't real gold, of course, and daddy knows I only wear real gold. If I wore this cheap thing my wrist would turn green.

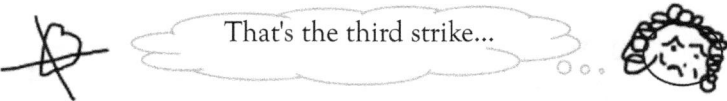

Do As I Say...

> **MOMMY, can I have a cookie?**

MAY I. No, it's too close to supper. It will spoil your appetite.

> **But I saw you have two!**

That's because I'm the grownup and you're the child.

> **What's that got to do with it?**

It means that I'm the boss here and there's no dessert for you tonight!

> *Someday I'LL be the boss...*

Vaccination

Self-Defense on the Playground

Beauty Lesson

Mommy, what are you doing?

Dying my hair blonde.

Why?

So I don't look old, like Grandma.

Grandma has pretty silver hair.

Yes, but silver hair is old. Like wrinkly skin. When my skin gets wrinkly I'll have a face lift. When you get older you'll understand. You have to suffer to be beautiful.

Will I have to dye my hair when it gets silver?

Of course! You can even dye your hair a better color than that muddy brown you've got. You could go blonde like me! And we can get your nose bobbed, maybe for your 16th birthday. And contacts if you'd rather have blue eyes, or maybe green instead of that watery hazel. Don't worry, we'll fix you up.

I guess I'm not so pretty - good thing my mom knows what to do.

Fairy Tale

There's just one way to end a fairy tale—
You know it as well as you know your name. *And then*
they lived happily ever after. Not simply "a happy ending,"
the romcom movie, the Harlequin book, where
our heroes find happiness on the last scene/page. The End.
But we, the audience, the readers, know, like Christmas,
like graduation, like the wedding day, the Best Day Of Your Life
will be gone with sunrise. No, the *ever after* is the magic trope,
the foreverness we guard (in secret) is make believe. Oh how
we must, we simply must bequeath it to our children, although it's doomed
to disappear with Santa Claus. And we who love them are their forever liars.
Out of love, we gave them *let's pretend.* They smile false smiles
at us. Yes mommy. Yes daddy. And we pay for it for the rest of their lives.

NOT Happily Ever After

Daddy daddy, Carol says Gerry Gerbil died! He was just lying in his cage and he wasn't doing anything, and her daddy said he died!

That's too bad, honey, she will be very sad for a while. But she can get another gerbil later.

But another gerbil won't be Gerry! Why did he die?

I don't know, maybe he just was very old, like that cactus we had, it just died because it was old. And then we got another one.

Grandma is very old. Is she going to die soon?

I don't think so, she is very healthy.

So was Gerry! He wasn't sick! If grandma dies, will we get another grandma?

No, it doesn't work that way. We will just be sad because she isn't here, but we will know her soul is in heaven and she is looking down on us and smiling at us. So that will make us happy.

What's a soul?

It's—it's—It's hard to explain. If they are good, they go to heaven/ What's heaven?/ Ask our minister, she knows more about that.

I won't be happy, never mind that soul, I want grandma! If she has to die and live in heaven, I want her to come back for my birthday. And Thanksgiving. I'm gonna tell her that right now.

That's enough of that, Grandma doesn't want to talk about it, it isn't nice to talk about people dying. Let's go eat lunch.

EVERYONE'S GONNA DIE—the plant, and the mosquito I hit, and Mommy and Daddy, and Tabby, and Carol and ME!

I don't like this AT ALL!

He loves me, he loves me not

> Oh stop bothering me! Go play in traffic.

♥ But everyone says children should play on the sidewalk and stay off the street so they don't get hit by a car. Does daddy want me to get hit by a car? ♥̶

An Unbelievable Scene That Happened (Part 1)

(how often? Who knows.)

See that sign? It says SAINT ANNE'S HOME FOR ORPHANS. I've had it with you. Your daddy's in the car, and he's gonna drive away with me. You just sit here on the steps. I won't be coming back.

(Time passes) (Door opens)

Hello, little girl, what's your name? Did you lose your mommy?

> My name is Kristen.
> My mommy doesn't want me.

Well, just come on in, Kristen, do you know your phone number? She must have been in a bad mood—I'm sure she'll want you back.

> NO, NO! I don't want to go back!

> Can you get my little brother out too?

READER: How does this story end? Perhaps you know.

>

An Unbelievable Scene That Happened (Part 2)

Hello, Sister, I'm Kristen's mom. Thanks for taking care of her.
I'll take her home now. I hope she didn't give you any trouble.
She can be such a willful wicked girl.

Really? No trouble at all. We think she is a lovely child.
But of course she was very upset that you left her here.
She thought you were never coming back.

Well naturally I would come back. Beatings didn't work.
I thought maybe I can scare the devil out of her. Can you imagine,
last night she spat out the spinach because she didn't like it.
I cook dinner, she has to eat it. Period.

I'll go and get her for you—have you considered getting
some help at home with your kids? Being a mom can be
very stressful.

NONE OF YOUR BUSINESS, thank you very much.
Just go get her!

NO No no no no no

First Day of Kindergarten

> Remember, don't talk to strangers.

But mommy, don't I have to say hello to the bus driver?

> That's different.

And my teacher?

> Yes, that's different, she's your teacher.

And what about the kids? I don't KNOW ANYONE BUT MARCY

> Forget it! I can't believe you are SO DUMB!

Teaching Generosity

This year we aren't going to have presents for Christmas. We really don't need anything. So Daddy and I decided we are going to take all the money we would have spent on gifts we don't need and send it to the starving children in Afghanistan.

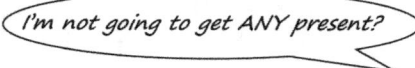

Well, if you want a present, we will get it for you, but some poor child will not have enough to eat! You are five years old, you are old enough to understand what is the right thing to do. It's your decision.

You know that's just a silly game. You are too old to believe in Santa Claus!

We'll all discuss it again next year. Now go outside and play.

54

Friend

Guess who's coming for lunch today? 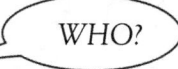 WHO?

Your cousin Andy! And after lunch you can both play with your new Lego set..

> I don't like Andy.
> He calls me PIPSQUEAK, and he kicks me when you aren't looking!

Of course you like him! He's FAMILY!
I don't want to hear another word about it.
Just play nicely and share your Lego.

> I pick my friends because I like them.
> I don't pick my family, so why do I
> have to like THEM when I don't!

Freedom of Choice

Eat your dinner before it gets cold.
What is it?

Chicken pot pie.
Is that with chicken?

Of course, silly. And vegetables and pie crust.
I will eat the vegetables and the pot pie crust.

What's the matter with the chicken!
It got killed—it used to walk around saying cluck cluck and laying eggs until someone killed it so we could eat it for dinner.

That's just the way it works—cows make steaks and burgers, pigs make pork, ducks make—duck...

I'm not eating dead animals or dead fish or dead birds. PERIOD!

She has a good point—but I like my dinners.

A Day Off From School

9am

> So can I stay home from school today?

Yes, you do have a temp, so no running around.

> Can I watch videos and cartoons?

Yes, I'll help make a playlist for you.

> COOL!

I have to work on Zoom for a while—see you at lunch!

9:30am   10am   10:30am

(THIS IS GREAT!)   *(What should I watch next?)*

11:00am

> DADDY, I'M BORED. THIS STUFF IS DUMB!

(IT WORKED!)

TAKE OUT SOME BOOKS! OR A BOX OF LEGO. I'm on a meeting!

(Lego! Books! I forgot!)

Ethical Dilemma (Age 6)

Learning My Colors at Breakfast

Reader—This page needs colors!
This page needs YOU!
Grab your crayons and get to work!

My friend Keisha says she is BLACK

But I think she is BROWN

And Carlos says he is BROWN.
But I think he is GOLD.

And they both say I am WHITE.

But I am NOT WHITE, I am sorta PINK.

So I am all mixed up!

Forget it. Just agree that you are white. Now finish your cereal.

Timing

Social Worker: You should really tell your daughter that she is adopted.
Parent: But won't she be upset that her mother gave her away?
Social Worker: Not if you emphasize how much you love her, how you chose her because she was just the baby you wanted.

So you know how we have blond curly hair and you have beautiful black straight hair?

> yes

And we have blue eyes and you have brown eyes?

> yes

That's because you are adopted!

> I know. I was Korean when I was a baby.

Who told you that?

> Oh, lots of people. Everyone asks me to say something in Korean. So silly. I was just a baby.

Yes, you were the sweetest baby, we loved you right away, so we took you home to be our baby. We named you Jin because that means jewel!

> Uh huh

Did you want to know anything else about how you were born?

> Nope. Can I ask Sara for a sleepover tonight?

Sure.

> *(I guess that went ok...)*

Sticks and Stones

Hey, hon, what's the matter?

LUISA CALLED ME A DUMMY.

Remember when we talked about that sticks and stones thing? She's being mean, and that isn't nice, but she didn't hit you.

BUT SHE HURT MY FEELINGS

The trick is to "take it from whom it comes." My mother taught me that, And I still follow her advice when someone insults me.

That doesn't really help, that WHOM was Luisa, who was my FRIEND!

I sure am glad I'm not seven years old anymore!

Introduction to Religion

(reading from the Bible): "In the beginning God created the heavens and the earth."
And...

Lots of people have asked that question. God just was always there! He didn't have to be created.

When you get older you won't worry about that.

> And who says God is a he!

Lots of people argue about that too, but can you imagine a she up in heaven doing all that creating?

> YES! You mustn't know a lot of women like my mommy. My mommy created me and my brother, and she creates lots of things all the time. Like dinners!

Well, let's call it a day. Maybe another time, when you are a few years older....

The Teacher Is Always Right

What happened to your pants?
Were you in a fight at school?

NO! The teacher hit me cuz/

NO EXCUSES YOUNG MAN!

If the teacher hit you she must have had a good reason.
You're going to get a beating when your father comes home.

Preparation for Life

"What's this call I got that you were caught stealing at the Stop & Shop?"

"Only fools get caught!"

OH NOW I GET IT!

Better be more careful next time...

Attachment, Scrambled

Fame/Honor/Glory/Death

Today, children, we honor Martin Luther King. How many of you have heard of him?
Yes, today is Martin Luther King Day, and we are going to talk about what he did and what he said. What do you children know about him?

He was an African American like me!

He said "I have a dream."

He was a minister.

CIVIL RIGHTS

NO VIOLENCE

Wouldn't it be wonderful if we could all be like Martin Luther King! Brave, and peaceful, someone who inspired others to do good things. A GREAT man.

AND THEN HE WAS MURDERED!!

Yes, that was so sad. Let's be quiet now, and just think of him.

I DON'T WANT TO BE GREAT AND GET MURDERED!

Always Tell the Truth #6: Home Alone

Addie, I'm going next door to talk to Mrs. Huxtable for a few minutes, if you want to call me just use this phone. You just press the picture of me, and I will answer it. OK?

Sure Mommy, that will be fun, can I try it now?

Sure, but only call me if you need to tell me something, not to play with it. I'll let you play with it again when I come home.

It will be fun to be home alone! I can pretend I am YOU!

There are a few rules—No touching the stove. No climbing on anything. OK?/OK/and don't answer the doorbell, and if you answer the phone and someone wants to talk to me, DO NOT SAY I AM NOT HOME. Just say, Mommy is on another phone, so please call back later.

But that isn't true! Isn't that a lie?

Oh GOD—yes, but it's like not telling someone about a present, it is a special kind of lie that is ok.

OK Mommy, I will do it the way you said.

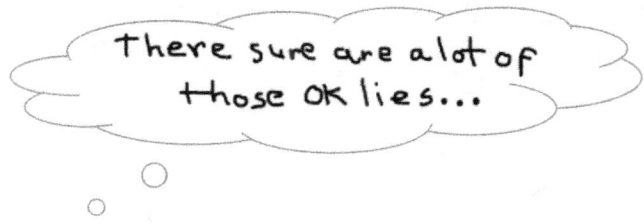

Those Who Are 10 Are Not 40.
Those Who Are 40 Are Not 10.

DAD! I DIDN'T MAKE THE BASKETBALL TEAM AGAIN!

Mostly it's the tall kids, right?

YEAH...

Face it, kid, you're not going to be tall. Your family comes from Guatemala, and people are short in Guatemala, like me and your mother and your brothers. But there are better sports anyway. Yeah, sports where you don't need a team.

LIKE WHAT?

Swimming! Running! Biking! Skating! Tennis! Skiing! Golf! Lots of things, and lots of them have races and other competitions. And you can do any of them without being picked for a team. So when you get to my age or even very old, like grandpa, you can play by yourself, or with friends, get your exercise and have some fun. The thing is to PRACTICE NOW so you can do it THEN!

When I get to his age... NO WAY!

No point in talking to him. Too bad 10 year olds can't get how it is at 40....

Bully

God, #1

> *Did you know that Mr. Martin got cancer? A really bad one— he will probably die soon.*

> Oh that's TERRIBLE! Johnny won't have a daddy. Why did God let that happen?

> *It's all for the best. Mr. Martin must have sinned greatly.*

> I don't think that's nice of God.

> *Don't say that! Remember what you were taught —"the wages of sin are death!"*

> Something's wrong with this... what about forgiveness?

God, #2

> Did you know that Mr. Martin got cancer? A really bad one— he will probably die soon.

> Oh that's TERRIBLE! Johnny won't have a daddy. Why did God let that happen?

> It's all for the best. Mr. Martin must have sinned greatly. He might end up going to Hell!

> Wow! Johnny might have learned to be a sinner like him.

> I'm glad you understand. Maybe you will grow up to be a priest, like Uncle Jack! You can pray for Johnny, that he understands how God is taking care of him.

> yes I will! And I'll tell Johnny how lucky he really is.

Justice

What? How can you tell such a lie about Father Jack! Such a holy man! You'll be damned to Hell! You better confess to Father Jack, right now! And pray for God's forgiveness.

Attempted Rape

It must have been your fault—
What were you wearing? That short skirt?

NO!

But I was wearing my new sneakers—was that why?

Studying the Constitution

All men are created equal.

Is that really true? Some men are tall and some are short, that's not equal… some are rich and some are poor, that's not equal…some are disabled… some are born deaf, or blind… so what does 'created equal' mean? [It's about their rights as human beings, that all men have equal rights in this country.] What about women? [Of course women are included.] Women aren't mentioned so they are not equal to men who are mentioned. **I DON'T THINK THAT'S RIGHT!** *It should say,* **"All humans are created equal."**

SIT DOWN! You are just being argumentative. Any more of that and I will send you to the principal's office.

Genes at the Passover Seder

Dad, why do we always drink grape juice instead of wine, like everyone else?

Grapes, wine, it's the "fruit of the vine," same thing.

Yes, but WHY don't we use wine?

That's a long story.

??

Ok, I suppose you are old enough. My father, Grandpa Lou, who died before you were born, he was an alcoholic. You know what that is?

Yeah, Patty's father is an alcoholic, and Jason's mother—

I can tell you it was terrible being the son of a drunk. Probably in my genes. Yours too. So if I were you I would stay away from it.

Patty drinks and Jason drinks—I think Patty drinks a LOT! Oh my god, what am I going to do in college! Everybody drinks in college. I'm gonna have to say I can't drink?

You'll get through it, I did, you'll be king of the designated drivers.

Oh no I just wanna be one of the guys....

And what do JEANS have to do with it?

Avoidant Attachment Disorder: A Simple Illustration

The boys were teasing the girls.
The usual *nyah nyah nyah*, the usual
doll-snatching, The usual torture, one boy
tossing the doll like a football, swinging her
by one cotton leg, round and round to achieve
the right spin. One girl crying—her baby,
of course—chasing the perpetrator, no chance
she'd catch him dancing and dodging between his pals.
Her face grimy, streaked with tears, her clothes
wet with sweat, she gives up, gasping, defeated
and stumbles towards her apartment house.

I'M GOING HOME TO MY MOTHER! *she sobs.*

Someone is thinking, so loudly you can almost hear it:

Why would she do THAT?

Reputation

I don't feel well.
I don't want to go to school today.

YOU GOT A TEST TODAY?

No, no tests—I just gotta BAD FEELING.

?

On Facebook—Billy's always writing about guns
and bombs—

!! DOES THE PRINCIPAL KNOW?

Of course not, he doesn't read those posts, he's OLD.

WE'RE GOING TO CALL THE POLICE, AND THEN WE'RE
GOING TO CALL THE PRINCIPAL, AND THEN–

But Mom, everyone will call me a SNITCH!

Said Without Thinking, Thinking Without Saying

78

A Slippery Definition

How come you drink so much?

I don't drink much—just this one glass a day before supper.

That's a BIG GLASS!

Yes, but half of it is soda. It's a cocktail.

Ethan says his mom is an alcoholic. She goes to AA.

I am not an alcoholic

Ethan says that's what all alcoholics say when they are drinking.

And that is what people say if they are not alcoholics!

¿ So how do you know ?

Scripture

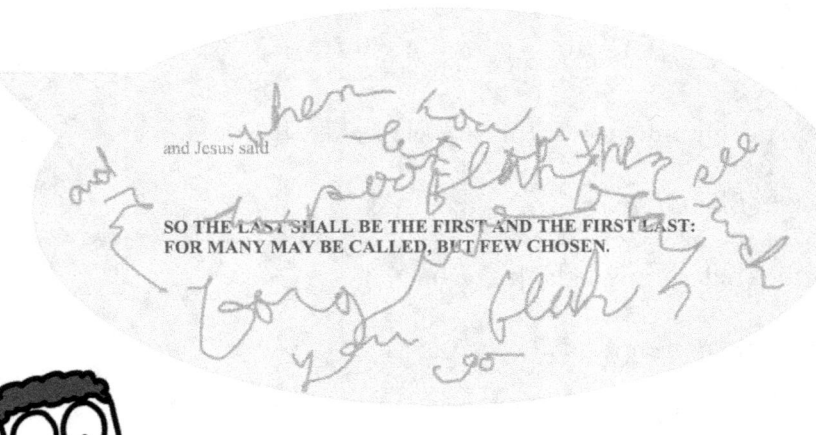

and Jesus said

SO THE LAST SHALL BE THE FIRST AND THE FIRST LAST: FOR MANY MAY BE CALLED, BUT FEW CHOSEN.

Dad, do you think Jesus was talking about me?
Like maybe I could someday be chosen first for the football team?

Look kid, give it up, football isn't for you.
How about the robotics team?

WHAT'S THE POINT OF RELIGION ANYWAY?

Father-Son Lecture

You know how Important it is to lead a clean life.   YES, DAD
And respect your body   YES, DAD
And respect the woman in your life   YES, DAD

Because The Lord is always watching you
Even your thoughts and your dreams
You may think no one knows what's in your heart
But He knows.   YES, DAD

So anytime you are tempted, remember
what I told you.   YES, DAD

and where you keep your passwords to the porn sites you watch...

Always Tell the Truth #7: (Not) Just What I Wanted

Happy Birthday, darling! I hope you like this little toy monkey!

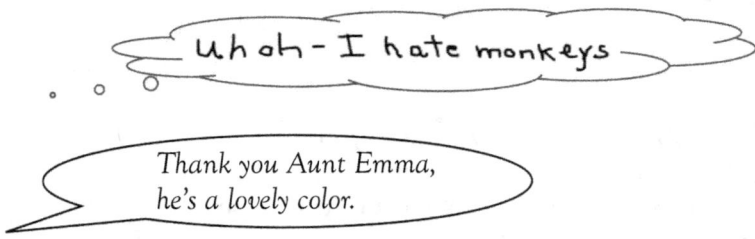

Thank you Aunt Emma, he's a lovely color.

I'm so glad you like him! I didn't know if you would rather have a doll.

I have dolls but I didn't have a monkey.

TIME FOR CAKE!

Music Class

Now children, we're all going to sing The Star Spangled Banner. It is a very hard song to sing because it goes very high, and requires holding your breath for a long time.

Here we go—oooh say can you see

STOP! I KNOW WHAT *I* SEE! MARTIN, WHAT'S THAT PIECE OF PAPER I SAW YOU HIDING? BRING IT UP HERE. READ IT OUT LOUD TO EVERYONE.

Ms. abbott is a witch.

LOUDER! *Ms. Abbott is a WITCH!*

So now, Martin, even though we know your voice is cracking, I know you will enjoy singing something special for us. This time when we sing The Star Spangled Banner, when we get to And the rockets red glare, the bombs bursting in air YOU WILL SING THOSE LINES ALONE! YOU WILL HAVE THE SOLO!

And now say Thank you Ms Abbott—

Tattling

I saw Wendy copying Zoe's math test.

That's the teacher's problem, not yours. MYOB.

I saw Bobby stealing candy at Target.

That's the store manager's problem, not yours. MYOB.

Pete signed his dad's name on the permission slip.

That's his dad's problem. MYOB.

Jackie's mom gets drunk every Sunday and hits the kids.

That's the dad's problem. MYOB.

Someone told me he is going to kill himself and he made me promise not to tell anyone.

THAT'S DIFFERENT, YOU HAVE TO TELL, WHO IS IT, THAT IS OUR BUSINESS!

HOW COME? YOU TOLD ME TO NEVER BREAK A PROMISE!

The Perils of Being Praised by the Teacher

You girls are teens now. It's time to eat healthy!
Do you want to get fat? You know who I'm talking to!
YES YOU! Do you want to have bad teeth?
And your SKIN! Pimples pimples pimples,
that's what I see on almost every face—

o god she's looking at me

that's me!

THAT'S ME!

EXCEPT MAGGIE! LOOK AT MAGGIE!
Maggie has beautiful smooth skin.
She hasn't got a single pimple.
And you know why that is, girls? SHE NEVER EATS CANDY!
SHE DOESN'T EAT CHOCOLATE! She cares
about her health!

OH MY GOD I WANT TO DIE ! PLEASE GOD, GIVE ME SOME PIMPLES ! PLEASE !

Secret Wishes

Sometimes I wonder why I wanted you at all, why can't you be like your brother he never gives me any trouble he gets A's in math and practices his piano without my nagging him and he comes right home from school and he doesn't lose his glasses and he eats all his supper without complaining and

ALL YOU DO IS CAUSE ME TROUBLE!

YOU'RE going to be the DEATH of me!

Last week you were late and you forgot to… the dentist… I had… appointment and you left your glasses… maybe they could have gotten broken…

I know you're nice, but sometimes I do wish…

Lesson From the Coach: How To Score

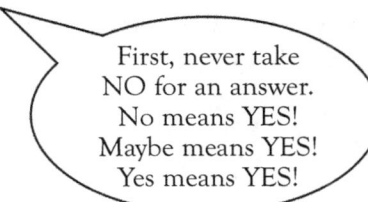

First, never take NO for an answer.
No means YES!
Maybe means YES!
Yes means YES!

WHAT MEANS NO?

Not Coming Out

Hey, Mark, I just heard, you know the Reverend's son Larry, he's gay.

(So am I)

Yeah, dad, I know.

Wow, I never would have guessed. On the football team and all. Boy, his dad must be frosted! What a scandal!

Mmm.

I sure am lucky, I don't know what I'd do. It's so disgusting! Y'know? Two guys— Gross!

(Keep that stoneface)

Mmm. Gotta go now, dad, hockey practice.

Glad you decided on hockey, you don't hafta run into Larry in a locker room, ha ha. No one like that on hockey, is there?

Dunno, Dad.

(there's me...) *(Better wait til college— far far away)* *(Send a text..?)*

Coming of Age

> *Hey, Mom, I have a really BIG Problem!*

Hey, sweetie, what's up?

> *This kid signed up to try out for pianist in the Spring musical. No one wants her—him? In the cast—She—or he?—looks really weird. And smells bad too. So they're figuring out how to make him—or her—ineligible to audition.*

So what's the problem for you?

> *I don't think that's right! The best pianist should win.*

If you say that you're toast. Didn't you want to run for Class President next term?

> THAT'S the problem!

**NO PROBLEM! NOT YOUR CIRCUS NOT YOUR MONKEY!
That means NONE OF YOUR BUSINESS, YOU NUMBSKULL!**

> *WHAT IT MEANS IS THAT I STILL HAVE A BIG PROBLEM.*

Being Beautiful

What's the matter, sweetheart? Why are you crying?

Laurie gets two dates every weekend, and I get NONE!

OH MY!

She is just so pretty.

Well, that is true. She looks like your mother. But don't cry, honey, that's just the way the genes went.
She got the beauty gene, and YOU got the brains!
Why are you crying now?

Did I say the wrong thing?

Is anyone ever going to think I'm pretty?

Maternal Advice

"I'm going out with Alan tonight!"

"Alan? That's the one who want to join the Peace Corps and teach a bunch of savages halfway around the world."

"Don't say I didn't warn you."

"But Ma"

"Get yourself a dentist, or an accountant. Or a computer guy. Who comes home for dinner every night. You could save up and pretty soon you can apply for a studio at Co-Op City!"

"OK, Ma, thanks, Ma"

Over my dead body!

Soap Opera Meets Real Life

Noon

(some Jewish holiday again, all the Jewish kids out, most of the teachers out, all the kids end up in study hall all day, what a waste of time, a great day to look around downtown. There's that new hotel, what a lobby! With that fancy bar off to the side, those bald guys with the gorgeous girls on their arms, bet those girls are half their age—)

WAIT — THAT'S MY DAD!

(What if he saw me! Oh will I be in trouble.)

6 PM

Hello, dear (KISS), how was the office today?

As usual, no time to go anywhere for lunch, had to eat at my desk.

You work much too hard, dear.
And how was school, Brian?

BOR-ING. Jewish holiday—just a few students and almost no teachers. All day in study hall. Waste of time.

Well, at least we'll all have a nice dinner together. Let's say the blessing. Oh Lord we thank you for this food. Amen.

The Facts of Life

Surprise

I have a very important announcement to make, so I want both of you to sit down and listen.

I am applying to a college in Australia / ! / Now just listen! You know how I was always interested in being a vet, but I really wasn't so interested in dogs and cats type animals, I wanted to work with giraffes! Elephants! Horses! Lions! All the big guys. And Australia has pre-vet and vet programs in Large Animals. That's what I want. And I can apply for a scholarship for transportation because they never have enough foreign students, and they really want to train people all over the world. I know you don't want me to go so far away, but it's really for a good reason.

That's a great idea! We're so excited for you!

You can come and visit too. Didn't you always want to see Australia?

Endpaper

> Well, Dr. Eliot, since this is our last session before I head off to college, I've been thinking about the rest of my life...

> MMM?

> Yes, I decided that I won't have any problem figuring out how to be a good parent when I have children some day.

> MMM?

> It'll be easy! I just will do the opposite of whatever my parents did! Then I'll be free of them at last.

> Well, no— because you will always be thinking of them, remembering what they did to make sure your decisions are the opposite of theirs! And you may even be startled to find that your behaviors are— Oh horror—the same!

OH NO!!

> Can I come back to see you if I want to, when I'm a parent I mean?

YOU

You're walking down the sidewalk, glancing
at the storefront windows—this bakery, that clothing store,
a sandwich shop—when suddenly you see a person
dressed just as you are. The same cap, the very same
jacket—you realize, laughing perhaps, that person is YOU,
YOU, grownup you whose hair is greyish, yes, of course
it's you. No longer the you who was afraid of the dark,
or the you who thought your kindergarten teacher was so old—
she was, you learned just recently, a mere 25.

Perhaps you've met yourself today, in these pages. Perhaps
you've gasped with recognition on one page, but not another.
You might have cried. Or shook with anger. Or spoke aloud
to the parent, or the kid, trying to explain, to offer the perspective
you've attained. After all, you made it through. Perhaps you've thought
What can I do to make a difference in this world where pain is passed
down like an old relic that remains up on the mantel, dusted weekly.

What do YOU say? I'm listening.

About the Author

Photo by Steven Shapiro

Having grown up in a housing project in The Bronx, Marian Kaplun Shapiro is delighted to be practicing as a psychologist from her home office in Lexington, Massachusetts, looking out on woods, flowers, birds, and unpolluted sky. She attended the then free Queens College, where she received her B.A. in English with a minor in music, and studied writing with Stanley Kunitz and Stephen Stepanchev. At 20 she married her astrophysicist husband and attended Harvard for a Masters in Teaching and English, studying poetry writing with Archibald MacLeish.

Teaching, two children, teaching again and then a return to Harvard for a doctorate in Psychology, culminated in a private practice as a psychologist, which she still pursues. In her forties she returned to writing: first, a professional book, next articles and chapters in psychology textbooks, and then a deep dive into poetry, resulting in approximately 450 publications, two books (*At the Edge of the Cliff: poems*, Plain View Press 2021 and *Players In The Dream, Dreamers In The Play*, Plain View Press 2007), and two chapbooks. Working with victims of violence, she recognized that in her heart she was a Quaker, and joined the Society of Friends, which holds an important place in her life and poetry. Now over 80, she is fortunate in loving and being loved by her adoring and adored husband, adult children, their spouses, and their five kind, funny, smart, talented, delightful children. Life to her is one long experiment, and she is unendingly grateful that hers has turned out so amazingly well.

www.ingramcontent.com/pod-product-compliance
Lightning Source LLC
Chambersburg PA
CBHW050039080526
44586CB00014B/1377